ANTHOLOGY

Royal Festival Hall
on the South Bank

sbc

Poetry Library

Royal Festival Hall, Level 5
London SE1 8XX
Telephone: 0171-921 0943

Books may be renewed by telephone

A Caribbean Dozen

For my Mother and Father – C.F.

Acknowledgements

The editors and publishers gratefully acknowledge permission
to use the following material:
By kind permission of John Agard c/o Caroline Sheldon Literary
Agency *Egg and Spoon Race* and *Ballad of Count Laughula* from
Laughter Is an Egg; published by Viking 1990. By kind permission
of Curtis Brown Ltd on behalf of Grace Nichols *For Dilberta*,
For Forest, *Ar-a-Rat* and *Sun Is Laughing*. *Isn't My Name Magical?*
© James Berry, 1994; reprinted by permission of the Peters Fraser
& Dunlop Group Ltd. *Bye Now*, *Letter From Your Special-Big-Puppy-Dog*
and *Letter From Your Kitten-Cat-Almost-Big-Cat* by James Berry from
When I Dance © James Berry 1988. First published by Hamish
Hamilton Children's Books 1988 and in Puffin Books 1990.
Chicken Dinner and *Ode to Twelve Chocolate Bars* © Valerie Bloom,
1992; reprinted by permission of Cambridge University Press from
Duppy Jamboree. *Remember* © Pamela Mordecai, 1987; reprinted by
permission of Ginn & Company Ltd from *Storypoems – A First
Collection*. *Morning Break*, *Charley and Miss Morley's Goat* and
Dancing Poinciana © Telcine Turner, 1977; reprinted by permission
of Macmillan Education Ltd from *Song of the Surreys*.
News © Telcine Turner, 1988; reprinted by permission of
Macmillan Caribbean from *Climbing Clouds*.

While every effort has been made to obtain permission, in some
cases it has been difficult to trace the copyright holders and we
would like to apologize for any apparent negligence.

First published 1994 by Walker Books Ltd
87 Vauxhall Walk, London SE11 5HJ

This edition published 1996

10 9 8 7 6 5 4 3 2

Photograph credits: Christine Voge (page 79),
Deo Persaud (page 55 and page 49)

This book has been typeset in Novarese.

Printed in Hong Kong

British Library Cataloguing in Publication Data
A catalogue record for this book is
available from the British Library.

ISBN 0-7445-5201-X

A CARIBBEAN DOZEN

A Collection of Poems

Edited by
John Agard and Grace Nichols

Illustrated by Cathie Felstead

WALKER BOOKS
AND SUBSIDIARIES
LONDON · BOSTON · SYDNEY

Contents

THE POETRY LIBRARY

Introduction
by John Agard and Grace Nichols

One of the things we recall about life in the Caribbean is the colourful, bustling markets, with their bargaining and bantering, and the way vendors would throw in an extra fruit or fish or handful of shrimps, especially if you had bought a lot. This bonus or extra bit of freeness is known around the Caribbean by various names such as the "mek-up" or the "brata". In keeping with this tradition, we have thrown an extra poet into your poetry basket – a generous Caribbean dozen of thirteen poets drawn from around the English-speaking Caribbean.

The voices of these poets are informed by the rhythms and flavours and textures of a Caribbean childhood. Though many of them now live in metropolitan places in Britain, Canada and the USA, their formative meeting with the magic of the word happened under tropical skies where fireflies were shooting stars and English nursery rhymes and fairytales mingled with the tricky doings of Anancy spiderman and ghost stories about duppies and jumbies with turned-back feet.

We've had great pleasure in putting these poets together and hope A *Caribbean Dozen* brings you dozens of delight.

Our house, in a small village in the middle of Jamaica, was full of children. I was the second of nine brothers and sisters, so there was always someone to play with. Various cousins came to live with us at one time or another, and this meant it was possible to play the ring games that needed six or more people. Best of all, though, I liked the skipping games, and I sometimes use the rhymes from these in my poems now. I was first introduced to poetry by my grandmother, mother and elder brother, while I was still at infant school. My brother would recite to me the poems he'd learnt at school and I loved it.

Valerie Bloom

My primary school was about four miles from home, but the roads were poor and sometimes there was no transport, so we would have a long walk. My favourite subject was English because I was good at it. I read a lot, and as soon as I started school I joined the local library. I can still remember the first book I borrowed – it was called Are You My Mother? and was about a baby chick looking for its mother. I enjoyed school but I enjoyed the holidays more, especially the eight weeks in summer when we could put hampers on our donkey and go into the hills to pick ripe mangoes. We would set off home, our hampers laden with fruit. For a couple of days we'd eat our fill, then we'd be off into the hills again. Bliss!

WATER EVERYWHERE

There's water on the ceiling,
And water on the wall,
There's water in the bedroom,
And water in the hall,
There's water on the landing,
And water on the stair,
Whenever Daddy takes a bath
There's water everywhere.

CHICKEN DINNER

Mama, don' do it, please,
Don' cook dat chicken fe dinner,
We know dat chicken from she hatch,
She is de only one in de batch
Dat de mongoose didn' catch,
Please don' cook her fe dinner.

Mama, don' do it, please,
Don' cook dat chicken fe dinner,
Yuh mean to tell mi yuh feget
Yuh promise her to we as a pet
She not even have a chance to lay yet
An yuh want to cook her fe dinner.

Mama, don' do it, please,
Don' cook dat chicken fe dinner,
Don' give Henrietta de chop,
Ah tell yuh what, we could swop,
We will get yuh one from de shop,
If yuh promise not to cook her fe dinner.

Mama, me really glad, yuh know,
Yuh never cook Henny fe dinner,
An she glad too, ah bet,
Oh Lawd, me suddenly feel upset,
Yuh don' suppose is somebody else pet
We eating now fe dinner?

LUCKY ME

Grass and carrots for the rabbit,
Seeds and grain for the turkey,
Some parboiled figs
Will do for the pigs,
But all the best foods for me.

One tiny hutch for the rabbit,
One little coop for the turkey,
I can't think why
Pigs love a sty,
But it's a nice big house for me.

They make a stew out of the rabbit,
And Christmas dinner from the turkey,
Pigs are taken
For ham and bacon,
But nobody dares eat me.

ODE TO TWELVE CHOCOLATE BARS

Oh glorious doz
That woz.

WHO DAT GIRL?

Who dat wide-eye likkle girl
Staring out at me?
Wid her hair in beads an' braids
An' skin like ebony?

Who dat girl, her eye dem bright
Like night-time peeny-wallie?
Wid Granny chain dem circle roun'
Her ankle, neck, an' knee?

Who dat girl in Mummy's shoes,
Waist tie wid Dad's hankie?
Who dat girl wid teeth like pearl
Who grinning out at me?

Who dat girl? Who dat girl?
Pretty as poetry?
Who dat girl in de lookin'-glass?

Yuh mean dat girl is me?

As a child I loved listening to folk tales told by the old people in our seaside village on the north coast of Trinidad. My grandmother was my favourite storyteller. She introduced me to the Bible and told me local, and other, nursery rhymes. She had a magical way of making stories and poems come alive. I cannot remember being taught to read and write; I guess they came as naturally to me as breathing. At primary and secondary schools I was always top of my class in essay writing and literature. I was good at reciting poetry too, and my teachers wanted me to enter the island-wide Recitation Contest — but at thirteen I was too shy. The subjects I had most difficulty with were maths and

Faustin Charles

science, and because I hated them I never worked very hard at them. The first books I fell in love with were Grimms' Fairy Tales, Andersen's Fairy Tales and The Town Mouse and the Country Mouse, which I received as a school prize. I began making up my own stories and poems from about the age of seven, telling them to my friends. I had my first essay accepted by a national Trinidad newspaper when I was twenty-two and my first book of poems was published four years later. I have since completed several more.

GREEN JEWELS

Suppose all the children
In the world turned green,
Green eyes, green hair, green colour!
Speaking in green voices everywhere;
The trees would be their mothers,
Summer would be their fathers,
And every night before they go to sleep
A black-eyed fairy will reap
Raindrops from their dreams
To keep them fresh and clean.

THE RUNNER

Run, run, runner man,
As fast as you can,
Faster than the speed of light,
Smoother than a bird in flight.
Run, run, runner man,
No one can catch the runner man,
Swifter than an arrow,
Outrunning his own shadow.
Run, run, runner man,
Faster than tomorrow.
Run, run, runner man,
Quicker than a rocket!
Into deep space spinning a comet!
Run, run, runner man,
Lighting the heavens of the night,
Run, run, runner man,
Out of sight,
Run, run, runner man, run!

STEEL BAND JUMP UP

I put my ear to the ground,
And I hear the steel-band sound:
Ping pong! Ping pong!
Music deep, rhythm sweet,
I'm dancing tracking the beat;
Like a seashell's ringing song,
Ping pong! Ping pong!
Moving along, moving along,
High and low, up and down,
Ping pong! Ping pong!
Pan beating singing, round and round,
Ping pong! Ping pong!

THE CAT WHO COULD FLY

Every night he flies from the window-sill,
Over the hill,
Purring dizzily at the full moon,
Circling the land, valleys, rivers and the sea;
Only thunder brings him down to earth
To an old lady's chamber.
In the daytime he sings sad songs,
And the world is silent,
For he cuts all tongues,
Sharper than a knife,
From miaowing the nine secrets of his life.

The cat who could fly,
Never told a lie
And drank all tears
From the old lady's eyes.

BRAZILIAN FOOTBALLER

Pelé kicked in his mother's belly!
And the world shouted:
Goooooooooooooooooooooooooooooooal!
When her son was born,
He became the sun,
And rolled on the fields of heaven.
The moon and stars trained and coached him,
In the milky way
He swayed, danced and dribbled,
Smooth like water off a duck's back
Ready always to attack.
One hot day, heaven fell down, floored!
Through the Almighty's hands
Pelé had scored!

I spent my small-girl days in a country village on the east coast of Guyana and my most treasured memory is of myself, around the age of six, standing calf-deep in goldish-brown water, watching fish go by just below the sunlit surface. When I was eight years old I moved with my five sisters, one brother, mother, father and grandmother to the city, Georgetown, with its white wooden buildings, bustling markets and famous St George's Cathedral (said to be the highest wooden building in the world). My father was a headmaster and my mother enjoyed playing the piano at home and loved having people around her. I can't remember a single day when our home wasn't visited

Grace Nichols

by friends or neighbours or relatives who had dropped in "just fuh a minute" but ended up staying hours, telling jokes and stories and sharing in whatever was cooked. I joined the Public Free Library when we moved to Georgetown and read my fill of Enid Blyton, William, Nancy Drew, and the Hardy Boys mysteries, much to the despair of our librarians who recommended other kinds of literature. But I did get a taste of "other literature", including poetry, from books at home. I can actually remember one of the first words I fell in love with — "excruciating"! I must have been about nine or ten, reading a William book in bed. William had just delivered a pinch under the table to some not-very-nice person's leg. The person shot up in "excruciating" pain. Apart from laughing, I remember savouring the sound of the word. I still get great pleasure from the sound of words.

FOR DILBERTA

(Biggest of the elephants at London Zoo)

The walking-whale
of the earth kingdom – Dilberta.

The one whose waist
your arms won't get around – Dilberta.

The mammoth one whose weight
you pray won't knock you to the ground.

The one who displays toes
like archway windows,
bringing the pads of her feet down
like giant paperweights
to keep the earth from shifting about.

Dilberta, rippling as she ambles under
the wrinkled tarpaulin of her skin,
casually throwing the arm of her nose,
saying, "Go on, have a stroke."

But sometimes, in her mind's eye,
Dilberta gets this idea – she could be a moth!
Yes, with the wind stirring behind her ears,
she could really fly.

Rising above the boundaries of the paddock,
Making for the dark light of the forest –
Hearing, O once more, the trumpets roar.

FOR FOREST

Forest could keep secrets
Forest could keep secrets

Forest tune in every day
to watersound and birdsound
Forest letting her hair down
to the teeming creeping of her forest-ground

But Forest don't broadcast her business
no Forest cover her business down
from sky and fast-eye sun
and when night come
and darkness wrap her like a gown
Forest is a bad dream woman

Forest dreaming about mountain
and when earth was young
Forest dreaming of the caress of gold
Forest roosting with mysterious eldorado

and when howler monkey
wake her up with howl
Forest just stretch and stir
to a new day of sound

but coming back to secrets
Forest could keep secrets
Forest could keep secrets
            And we must keep Forest

AR-A-RAT

I know a rat on Ararat,
He isn't thin, he isn't fat
Never been chased by any cat
Not that rat on Ararat.
He's sitting high on a mountain breeze,
Never tasted any cheese,
Never chewed up any old hat,
Not that rat on Ararat.
He just sits alone on a mountain breeze,
Wonders why the trees are green,
Ponders why the ground is flat,
O that rat on Ararat.
His eyes like saucers, glow in the dark –
The last to slip from Noah's ark.

29

SUN IS LAUGHING

This morning she got up
on the happy side of bed,
pulled back
the grey sky-curtains
and poked her head
through the blue window
of heaven,
her yellow laughter
spilling over,
falling broad across the grass,
brightening the washing on the line,
giving more shine
to the back of a ladybug
and buttering up all the world.

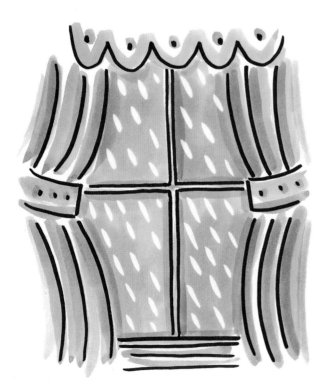

Then, without any warning,
as if she was suddenly bored,
or just got sulky
because she could hear no one
giving praise
to her shining ways,
Sun slammed the sky-window close,
plunging the whole world
into greyness once more.

O Sun, moody one,
how can we live
without the holiday of your face?

I grew up in the Bahamas. Milton Street, off Market Street, New Providence Island, was my birthplace. As a child I was sickly, and hence reserved. Comics, books and newspapers were my frequent companions, although I developed many lasting friendships. Pets I recall include Cluck-Cluck the hen, Princess the goat, Mixie the cat, and dogs Sundae, Maestro and Star. "Babylon", the yard where I spent much of my childhood and adolescence, would now be called a ghetto or slum, but at that time we weren't too conscious of such terms. Generally, my extended family and neighbours were friendly and witty. A golden wall loomed up along the northern side of

Telcine Turner

Babylon. It enclosed a wonderful place — a combination of movie theatre, nightclub and living quarters for the owner, a retired dancer who walked in the middle of the road like a god. It wasn't until his tragic death that we learned of his world-wide fame. As children we admired the fascinating murals, tiles and gardens in that forbidden golden mansion. It was the singing I heard from there along with songs played on the radio in the Fifties that ignited my interest in words and music.

NEWS

"Mummy, hey Mummy,
  bet you can't guess what happened
  right after I bathed off
  and shampooed my hair…"

"Good for you, dumpling.
  You're finished; that's something.
  Now you will need
  some pyjamas to wear."

"Mummy, oh Mummy,
  I can't wait to tell you –
  I combed out my hair
  then I brushed *all* my teeth…"

"I'm proud of you, precious,
  you do look delicious.
  Go to the drawer
  and get socks for your feet."

"Mummy, please Mummy,
  look here in my mouth.
  When I flossed like you told me
  my jaw tooth flew out!"

MORNING BREAK

Girls in white blouses, blue skirts,
boys in blue trousers, white shirts,
singing, swinging, screeching, reaching,
hooking wasps, riddle-saying,
ring-playing –

Bayhanna, bayhanna, bayhanna, bay.
If your teachers scold you
Listen to what they say.
That's the way you bayhanna, bayhanna, bay.

Lamppost schoolmaster in grey jacket,
grey tales of wild Abaco hog and donkey;
mild worry, calm hurry,
stiff bones and cane;
ring-playing –

Round the green apple tree
Where the grass grows so sweet,
Miss Della, Miss Della,
Your true lover was here,
And he wrote you a letter
To turn 'round your head.

First bell, all frozen.
Second bell, instant motion.
Disappear.

33

CHARLEY AND MISS MORLEY'S GOAT

Charley's mother went to town
Run, Charley, run
With a red hat on and a purple gown.
Run, Charley, run

Before she left she told the boys,
Run, Charley, run
"You all stay home and play with your toys."
Run, Charley, run

Charley's brother and sister too
Run, Charley, run
Cleaned up the yard. What did he do?
Run, Charley, run

He dashed with friends up and down the street.
Run, Charley, run
Then Miss Morley's goat they began to beat.
Run, Charley, run

The goat cried, "Ma-a-a!" Miss Morley woke.
Run, Charley, run
When she saw the boys she was vexed and spoke:
Run, Charley, run

"Why don't you leave my goat alone?"
 Run, Charley, run
"Charles, I'll tell your mother when she comes home."
 Run, Charley, run

Bad as her word, when the jitney brought Mom,
 Run, Charley, run
Miss Morley told her about her son.
 Run, Charley, run

Under the bed, Charley heard Mom say,
 Run, Charley, run
"I'm going to fix his skin today!"
 Run, Charley, run

"Come out here, Charles, and I mean RIGHT NOW."
 Run, Charley, run
"Who told you to leave this yard, anyhow?"
 Run, Charley, run

Charley was spanked and sent to bed
 Run, Charley, run
For not doing what his mama said.
 Run, Charley, run

DANCING POINCIANA

Fire in the treetops,
Fire in the sky.
Blossoms red as sunset
Dazzling to the eye.

Dance, Poinciana,
Sway, Poinciana,
On a sea of green.
Dance, Poinciana,
Sway, Poinciana,
Regal as a queen.

Fire in the treetops,
Fire in the sky.
Crimson petals and white
Stained with scarlet dye.

Dance, Poinciana,
Sway, Poinciana,
On a sea of green.
Dance, Poinciana,
Sway, Poinciana,
Regal as a queen.

I grew up on the banks of a wide river in Guyana in South America. Like all the other children on the river I learnt to swim and paddle a canoe at a very early age. We must have been very brave or else we didn't understand the dangers around us, for in that river and in the water places nearby were stingrays, alligators, electric eels and the largest snakes in the world — water boa constrictors, or "camudis" as we called them. One of them swallowed my grandfather's dog, Bunty, which was about the size of an Alsatian. In and around our house, on the river banks, there were wasps, scorpions, tarantulas and even snakes, and in the nearby forests, monkeys, baboons, tiger cats and jaguars. I survived all that and became a singer/songwriter and poet when I grew up.

David Campbell

With my guitar I travelled to many places including Sweden, England, Wales, Scotland, Ireland, Holland, Germany, the United States, Central America and right across the big country where I now live, Canada. I have made my home where the mountains meet the Pacific Ocean, in Vancouver. In this city you can see eagles soaring in the sky and mountain tops that are still wild. You can walk for miles by the ocean and through wide green places. I love living here.

CORN AND POTATO

The corn and potato, peanut, strawberry:
Who gave them to us, can anyone tell me?
Canoes and snowshoes, hammocks for swinging:
Where did they come from in the beginning?

Was it Wonder Woman? No, No,
Six Million Dollar Man? No, No, No,
Was it Tom and Jerry? No, No,
Sylvester and Tweety? No, No, No,
Then was it Max B. Nimble? No, No,
Rocky and Bullwinkle? No, No, No,
Then was it Spiderman? No, No,
It must be Superman! No, No, No, No, No!

Next time you eat your strawberry jam
And peanuts, just ask your daddy this question:
Where did these come from? I'll give you one clue:
It wasn't Archie Bunker, that's all I can tell you.

Was it Paul Bunyan? No, No,
Was it Abraham Lincoln? No, No, No,
Francisco Pizarro? No, No,
Was it Robinson Crusoe? No, No, No,
Was it a Pilgrim Father? No, No,
Or an old fur trader? No, No, No,
Columbus or Champlain? No, No,
Tennille and the Captain? No, No, No,
I give up, won't you tell me? Yes, Yes, Yes, Yes, Yes!

If you can't guess then I'd better tell you
Listen to me, I don't want to fool you
Before Columbus, before the Pilgrims,
These things and more all came from the Indians.

The Mic-Mac, the Sarcee, Yes, Yes,
Ojibway and Plains Cree, Yes, Yes, Yes,
The Sioux and the Cheyenne, Yes, Yes,
Apache and Peigan, Yes, Yes, Yes,
The Arawak or Taino, Yes, Yes,
The Mapuche, the Saulteaux, Yes, Yes, Yes,
The Hopi, the Haida, Yes, Yes,
The Inca, the Maya, Yes, Yes, Yes, Yes, Yes!
(I said Yes! Yes! Yes!)

39

ALL THE ONES THEY CALL LOWLY

Garter snake, garter snake, you hurt no one;
You move on so gracefully through the grass.
Garter snake, garter snake, I'll be your friend
And not run away as you pass.

Grasshopper, grasshopper, hopping so high
Away from our crazy feet close to you;
Grasshopper, grasshopper, I'll be your friend;
I wish I could hop as high as you.

Speckled frog, speckled frog, I like your pad;
I don't believe I'll catch warts from you.
Speckled frog, speckled frog, I'll be your friend;
Why should I be frightened of you?

Wriggly worm, wriggly worm, get back inside –
A robin is waiting to take you home;
Wriggly worm, wriggly worm, I'll be your friend;
Above ground you'll not be alone.

All the ones that they do call lowly,
That do no harm to you or me –
Each will be my secret buddy
On grass and water, sand and tree.

THE POW-WOW DRUM

Long black braids and silken shawls
Moving side by side where the eagle calls,
Answering the beat of the pow-wow drum
we come again
to dance again

Hey-a, Hey-a, Hey-a, Hey-a, Hey!
Hey-a, Hey-a, Hey-a, Hey-a, Hey!

Leave the dusty cities far behind,
Meet our brothers of the country with one mind,
Travelling from the east, north, south and west
we come again
to dance again

Chorus

Watching close the feet of lightning fly
Fancy dancers free underneath the sky,
Joining in the circle moving round and round
we come again
to dance again

Chorus

Women shining like the morning sun,
Children making rainbows as they laugh and run,
The old and young meeting like they did long ago
we come again
to dance again

Chorus

The sea has always been, and remains, important to me. As a child, my family went to the beach almost every Sunday. When I was thirteen my poem, "The Sounds I Like to Hear", was published and, not surprisingly, that poem talked about the sea. I grew up primarily on sugar estates, because my father was a chemist and worked in the sugar refineries converting cane juice into rum, and my mother was an executive secretary managing the estate offices. My older sister and I were very close and we got up to lots of mischief. There was always lots of open space where we lived and

Opal Palmer Adisa

there was nothing I loved more than running through the fields and among the tall grasses, then lying on my back and imagining different animals in the clouds. I spent many summers in a small village with my mother's relatives, and that experience is one that I'll never forget. My Aunt Zilla was a great teller of Duppy (ghost) and Anancy stories. Often, when she'd finished, especially if it was a dark, moonless night, I would be so scared I wouldn't move without someone walking with me. I seem to remember always writing, or at least making up stories and poems in my head. I still make up stories that I tell to my two daughters, Shola and Teju, and my son, Jawara. Now Shola, who is seven, is herself a great storyteller. I enjoy all sorts of writing, from academic essays, to poetry, to children's stories.

BEING A TREE

One time
I stood on the arm of the sofa
balancing on one leg
my arms spread wide
like branches.

I was a gigantic tree
in the deep green forest.
Many birds sat on my branches
chirping their happy songs.
Small animals nestled by my trunk
prancing and playing, being free.
And just as a blue jay
was about to land on my branch
Mom shouted, "Be careful!"
The blue jay flew away.
I fell, and my tree toppled over.

De More de Merrier

sitting on the
window-sill
looking down
on the street
watching folks
go by
wanting
to be there
in the midst
of it all
but stuck up
here all by myself
no friend
no sister
no brother
not even a dog
to talk to

mama off
somewhere
doing chores
papa still
at work

just me
all by myself
warned not to
go anywhere
told not
to let anyone in
not even a friend
especially if
he's a boy

rules
nothing but rules
not allowed
to choose
not allowed
to decide for myself

i guess
the more the merrier
only applies
to relatives
who come to visit
on holidays

FRUITS

mangoes
and ripe bananas
jelly coconut
and pomegranates
jack-fruit
and stinking-toe
june plum
and nase-berry
sweetsop
and sour-sop
tamarind
and jimbeli
cane-juice
and coolie-plum
star-apple
and custard-apple
navel orange
and wild cherries

fruits everywhere
brimming with life
spread out in front
of market women
buy some
and experience delight

I Am the One

I am the one
who comes out
after dark.
My loveliness
rarer than
a black rose.
With me beauty
is not merely skin deep.
My eyes
pool of deep ocean waters
glittering under the sun.

To others
I am a ray
on a cold bleak day
Forever a daffodil
Penetrating as a needle
Brilliant as diamond.

I dine
with the moon and stars
allowing them to gaze
at my grace.

I am fragrant jasmine
innovative as the traffic light
Ancient as Timbuktu.

Yes, I am the one
Cool and protective
I'm a child of the night .

My homeland is the South American country which the Arawak Indians named Guyana, "Place of Many Waters". We're part of the Caribbean, but we share gigantic rivers and rainforests with our continental neighbours, Brazil, Venezuela and Surinam. As a child I lived on the Berbice River at Bartica and later on the Demerara, which means "gold" and gives its name to the golden brown sugar and rum. I was born during the Second World War, a time of "Grow More Food" posters and battle news on the radio. While growing up I had all sorts of nicknames like Marco, Tallboy, Speedy, but to my family I was simply MC. My storehouse of

Marc Matthews

happy childhood memories includes family performances, plays, poetry recitals and singsongs, and my pets — a turtle called Criptocks and dogs called Paddy, Spliff and Cinco. One thing I will never forget is my return home from England after ten years and four letters away. I was riding through my old neighbourhood when the grandmother of my age-mate Hank leaned out of the window and shouted, "Mac'o, is you boy? Come here!" Then she sent a child to gather my old friends, and started the welcome party. The feeling I had then is the feeling I get now every time I hear the theme song from Cheers, "Where Everybody Knows Your Name".

BOATS

long boats and short boats
fat boats and narrow boats
boats with motors
boats with sails
boats with paddles
boats with steam

boats in rivers
boats in seas
boats in canals
boats in streams
boats made of wood
boats made of steel
boats made of skins
but none can beat
my boat made from
half a dry coconut
skin

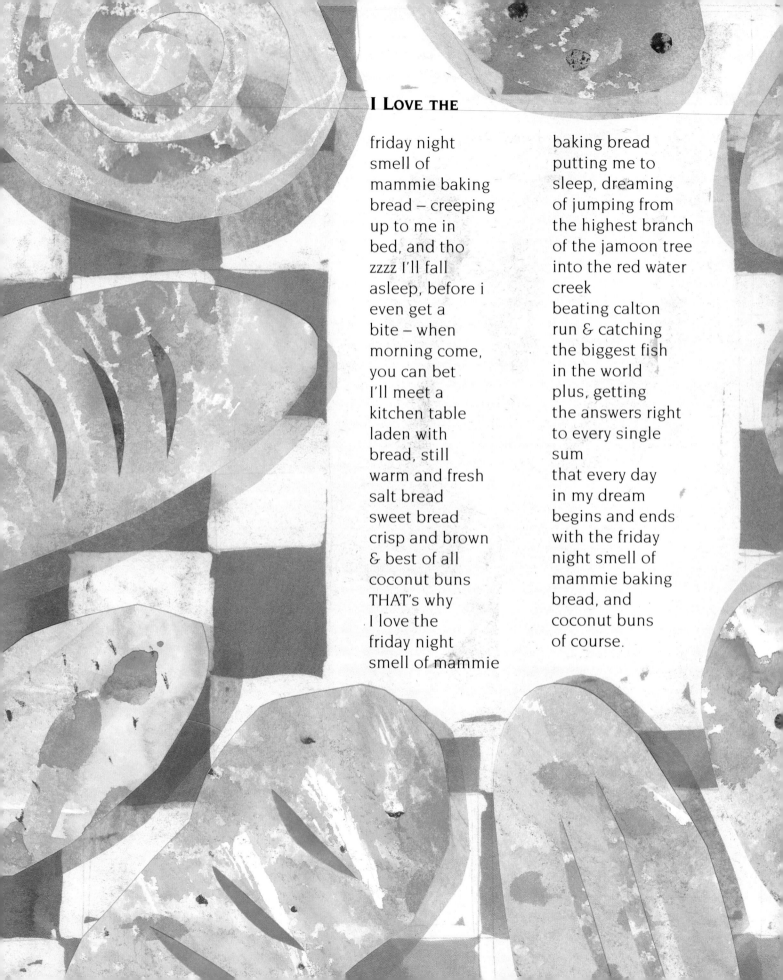

I LOVE THE

friday night
smell of
mammie baking
bread – creeping
up to me in
bed, and tho
zzzz I'll fall
asleep, before i
even get a
bite – when
morning come,
you can bet
I'll meet a
kitchen table
laden with
bread, still
warm and fresh
salt bread
sweet bread
crisp and brown
& best of all
coconut buns
THAT's why
I love the
friday night
smell of mammie

baking bread
putting me to
sleep, dreaming
of jumping from
the highest branch
of the jamoon tree
into the red water
creek
beating calton
run & catching
the biggest fish
in the world
plus, getting
the answers right
to every single
sum
that every day
in my dream
begins and ends
with the friday
night smell of
mammie baking
bread, and
coconut buns
of course.

ME AND MY BALL

Ball jump off of my window-sill
Ball jump off of the floor
Ball jump over granny chair
Ball jump off of the door
Ball jump into granny lap
Ball make granny stop snore

53

A SHOWER A SHAVE A SHAMPOO A CHIN

Sometimes in the bathroom
where I can't be seen
with Daddy's shaving brush
lather my face with his cream

take the razor from out of
his shaver, to shave myself
when I'm finished, with his
aftershave lotion wash my
face clean.

Then put on his favourite slippers
sit in his favourite chair, pick up
a big newspaper and make Mummy
burs' a laugh when I call out
"How about a cup of coffee out here,
my dear."

54

As a little boy I liked listening to cricket on the radio. I'd try to imitate the famous voice of the commentator, John Arlott. I'd make up pretend commentaries about a batsman hooking "majestically" and "magnificently", not realizing that I myself was becoming hooked on the sound of words. My primary school was called St Mary's and it faced a big Roman Catholic cathedral called Brickdam. The boys wore short khaki trousers with navy blue shirts, and the girls wore navy blue skirts with white sailor-collar tops. Since there was no winter, our teachers often took us outdoors, especially for subjects like drawing and nature study. I liked it when we went into the avenues lined with flamboyant, red-flowered trees,

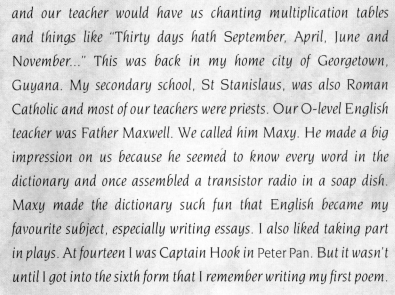

and our teacher would have us chanting multiplication tables and things like "Thirty days hath September, April, June and November..." This was back in my home city of Georgetown, Guyana. My secondary school, St Stanislaus, was also Roman Catholic and most of our teachers were priests. Our O-level English teacher was Father Maxwell. We called him Maxy. He made a big impression on us because he seemed to know every word in the dictionary and once assembled a transistor radio in a soap dish. Maxy made the dictionary such fun that English became my favourite subject, especially writing essays. I also liked taking part in plays. At fourteen I was Captain Hook in Peter Pan. But it wasn't until I got into the sixth form that I remember writing my first poem.

BALLAD OF COUNT LAUGHULA

Dead on the stroke of the midday bell
Count Laughula rises
from his merry shell.

Midday sky resounds with a crack
and Count Laughula plans
another side-splitting attack.

Draped in pudding-yellow cloak
that wobbles in the wind
Count Laughula sharpens a deadly joke.

This is a Count that does not haunt by night
but prefers to stalk a victim
in broad daylight.

When a judge throws off his wig and laughs HA-HA-HA
you can bet he's been bitten
by none other than Count Laughula.

When your teacher gets stitches in her side
and leans on the desk
you know she has been Count Laughula's bride.

When a Prime Minister demands a lollipop
in the middle of a speech
Count Laughula is surely getting on top.

He is the vampire that makes you laugh
and all over the city
he'd sign his mysterious autograph.

And when sun goes down, hook or crook,
Count Laughula returns to his shell
safely tucked in with a comic book.

WHAT THE TEACHER SAID WHEN ASKED:
WHAT ER WE AVIN FOR GEOGRAPHY, MISS?

This morning I've got too much energy
much too much for geography

I'm in a high mood
so class don't think me crude
but you can stuff latitude and longitude

I've had enough of the earth's crust
today I want to touch the clouds

Today I want to sing out loud
and tear all maps to shreds

I'm not settling for river beds
I want the sky and nothing less

Today I couldn't care if east turns west
Today I've got so much energy
I could do press-ups on the desk
but that won't take much out of me

Today I'll dance on the globe
in a rainbow robe

while you class remain seated
on your natural zone
with your pens and things
watching my contours grow wings

All right, class, see you later.
If the headmaster asks for me
say I'm a million dreaming degrees
beyond the equator

a million dreaming degrees
beyond the equator

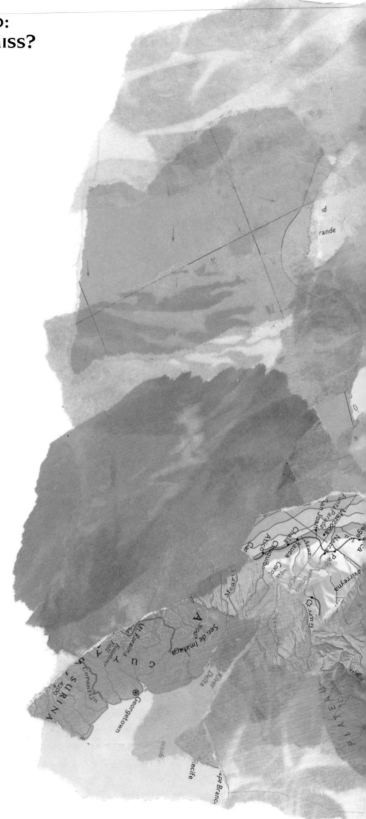

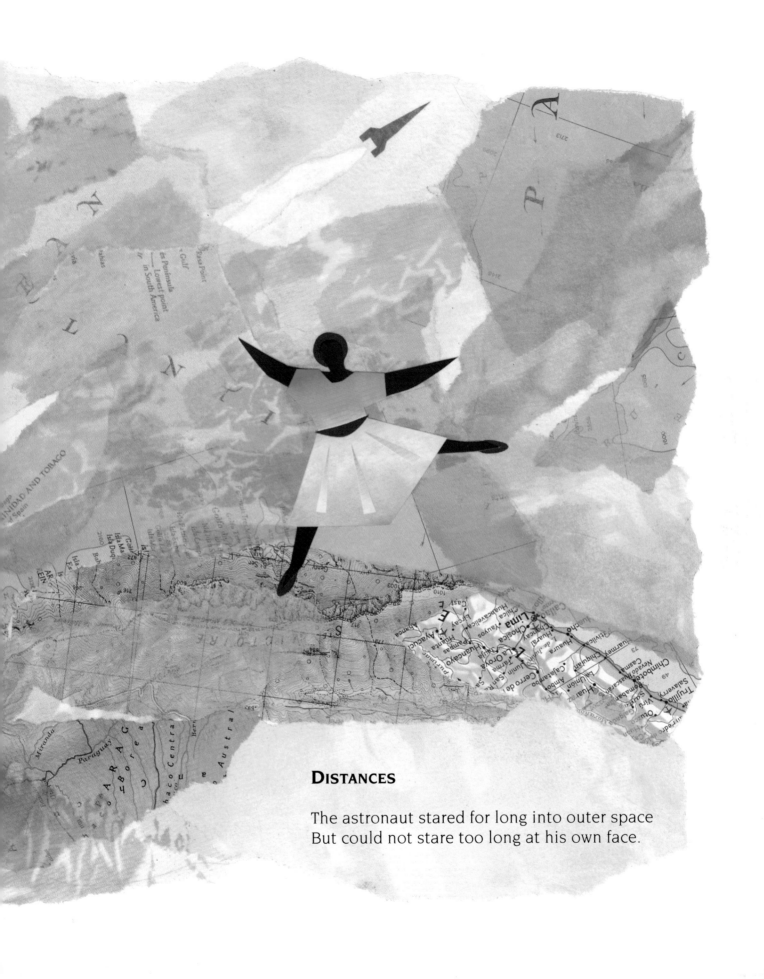

DISTANCES

The astronaut stared for long into outer space
But could not stare too long at his own face.

EGG-AND-SPOON RACE

One school sports day,
in the egg-and-spoon race,
    the egg ran away
    from the spoon.

The egg brought first place
but judges said: "Let's disqualify
the egg.
It should have waited on the spoon."

The egg said: "Why not disqualify
the spoon
for not catching up with me?
I'll never understand the mystery
    of the human race."

WHEN ANANCY SAY

When Anancy say walk
yuh better run

When Anancy say talk
yuh better dumb

When Anancy say come
yuh better go

When Anancy say quick
yuh better slow

When Anancy say wet
yuh better dry

When Anancy say true
yuh better lie

I was born deep in the south of Trinidad in a village called Guayguayare. Our house was so close to the ocean that when the tide came in the pillow tree logs on which the house stood were almost covered by surf. When I was four or so my grandmother, who brought me up, moved to San Fernando, but every holiday we would return to Guaya where my grandfather lived. It is the place I remember and love most. I now live in Toronto, Canada, but each time I go back to Trinidad I always go to Guayguayare just to see the ocean there, to breathe in the smell of copra drying and wood burning and fish frying. In the Sixties, when I was in elementary and high

Dionne Brand

schools, none of the books we studied were about Black people's lives; they were about Europeans, mostly the British. But I felt that Black people's experiences were as important and as valuable, and needed to be written down and read about. This is why I became a writer. In San Fernando I went to a girls' high school where I was taught that girls could use their intellect to live a full life. My teachers and friends there helped me to see that women should enjoy the same rights and freedoms as men. When I moved to Canada in 1970 I joined the civil rights, feminist and socialist movements. I was only seventeen but I already knew that to live freely in the world as a black woman I would have to involve myself in political action as well as writing.

SKIPPING ROPE SONG

Salt, vinegar, mustard, pepper,
If I dare,
I can do better,
who says no?
'cause hens don't crow!
Salt, vinegar, mustard, pepper.

Salt, vinegar, mustard, pepper.
I wanna be great,
a hotshot lawyer,
a famous dancer,
a tough operator,
Salt, vinegar, mustard, pepper.

Salt, vinegar, mustard, pepper,
If I dare
I can do better,
who cares from zero,
that hens don't crow,
Salt, vinegar, mustard, pepper.

RIVER

Take the clothes to the river
beat them on the stones
Sing some songs to the river
praise its deep green face
But don't go where river meets sea
there's a fight going on.
The fight is blue and green and gold,
the current is strong and foamy
'Cause river wants to go to sea
but sea won't be her boat.

62

WIND

I pulled a hummingbird out of the sky one day
but let it go,
I heard a song and carried it with me
on my cotton streamers,
I dropped it on an ocean and lifted up a wave
with my bare hands,
I made a whole canefield tremble and bend
as I ran by,
I pushed a soft cloud from here to there,
I hurried a stream along a pebbled path,
I scooped up a yard of dirt and hurled it
in the air,
I lifted a straw hat and sent it flying,
I broke a limb from a guava tree,
I became a breeze, bored and tired,
and hovered and hung and rustled and lay
where I could.

HURRICANE

Shut the windows
Bolt the doors
Big rain coming
Climbing up the mountain

Neighbours whisper
Dark clouds gather
Big rain coming
Climbing up the mountain

Gather in the clotheslines
Pull down the blinds
Big wind rising
Coming up the mountain

Branches falling
Raindrops flying
Treetops swaying
People running
Big wind blowing
Hurricane! on the mountain.

OLD MEN OF MAGIC

Old men of magic
with beards long and aged,
speak tales on evenings,
tales so entrancing,
we sit and listen,
to whispery secrets
about the earth and the heavens.
And late at night,
after sundown they speak
of spirits that live
in silk cotton trees,
of frightening shadows
that sneak through the dark,
and bright balls of fire
that fly in night air,
of shapes unimaginable,
we gasp and we gape,
then just as we're scared
old men of magic
wave hands rough and wrinkled
and all trace of fear disappears.

The raw salt smell of the sea and Christmas cakes baked in the big brick "outside" ovens, and ham and puddings boiled in kerosene tins in the backyard... These are some of my early memories of Kingston, Jamaica, where I grew up. I was born in my grandparents' house, next door to the police head-quarters and not far from the sea. I remember seeing at least one sea cow (manatee) beached there. Also, I remember it was a wonderful, very old house with a parlour, blinds, wooden floors and a huge open cellar, with a holly bush at the bottom of the stairs in front. It wasn't the house where we lived, but for me it will always be the house of

Pamela Mordecai

my childhood. Nearly every night before we went to bed, my father would read to us from The Best Loved Poems of the American People. *He still has the book, and now he's very ill I read him the same poems he used to read to us. The poems had wonderful rhymes and rhythms and some were very sad. I always say that if I write poetry "is my Daddy start it". At school I took part in the All-Island Poetry Competition organized by the Jamaica Poetry League, and learnt many Caribbean poems to recite – especially those of Louise Bennett-Coverley, Jamaica's great poet/actress, known as Miss Lou. I also say that if I write poetry "is because of Miss Lou". Inside I'm still about three and a half – which is maybe why I like writing poems and stories for children. I believe that God lives and speaks through poems and stories.*

REMEMBER

Remember when
the world was tall
and you were small
and legs were all
you saw?

Jumping legs
prancing legs
skipping legs
dancing legs.

Thin legs
fat legs
dog legs
cat legs.

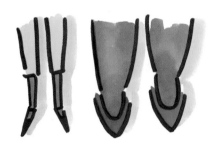

Shoes-and-sock legs
on the rocks legs.

Standing-very-tall legs
running-all-around legs.

Table legs
chair legs
dark legs
fair legs.

Stooping-very-small legs
lying-on-the-ground legs.

Quick legs
slow legs
nowhere-
to-go legs.

Remember when
the world was tall
and you were small
and legs were all
you saw?

RABBIT POEM

To keep
a rabbit
is a good
habit.

A rabbit is truly curious:
his eyes are soft
but his whiskers wiggle
and his nose twitches
and his ears jiggle

and his tail
is a bump
on
his rump.

A rabbit
is cheerful
but not especially
careful
about multiplying:
the answers
he gets
to the simple
sum
of one and one
are mystifying…

A rabbit is easy
to care for:
to munch on grass
is what he's hare for.

So if you get
the chance
to have a rabbit,
grab it!

LAMENT OF AN ARAWAK CHILD

Once I played with the hummingbirds
and sang songs to the sea
I told my secrets to the waves
and they told theirs to me.

Now there are no more hummingbirds
the sea's songs are all sad
for strange men came and took this land
and plundered all we had.

They made my people into slaves
they worked us to the bone
they battered us and tortured us
and laughed to hear us groan.

Today we'll take a long canoe
and set sail on the sea
we'll steer our journey by the stars
and find a new country.

QUAO

Quao
is a
lizard.
He is a
wizard
at catching
flies
and other
insects
of minimal
size
who happen
to fall
in his way.
If you are
small,
then,
it would

NOT
be wise
to go
near
Quao.

The first four years of my life were spent in the commercial quarter of Port-of-Spain, Trinidad, with all its bustle, noise and sharp smells. It was here that I saw my first carnival, which I found both frightening and exciting. The music seemed to enter my body; and Jab Molassi with his devil mask was horrifying. When I was about six we moved to the outskirts of the city where it was green and open, and where I really began to enjoy school. School for me then was play, poetry recitation, singing, drawing and nature study. All the other subjects were a bore. I loved the Caribbean folk tales and the poems in my Nelson Reader, many of which I had to learn by heart. On moonlit nights we scared each other with supernatural tales of La Diablesse, Soucouyant and the Jumbies. Encouraged by my Aunt Christine I discovered the wonderful world of books. Sir Walter Scott was one of my favourite authors. After reading Quentin Durward my grandma's healthy banana plant, laden with unripe fruit, suffered a fatal thrust of my wooden sword in a one-sided duel. It was, I believe, this desire to relive the adventures in the books I read that led me to write my first short story and eventually to become a writer and poet. But all those brightly-coloured illustrations from books in my early childhood gave me a love of art and design as well, which led me to become a painter.

John Lyons

THE PUM NA-NA FROGS

"Pum na-na,"
say the frogs
on a rainy season night
when the moon is bright.

"Pum, pum, pum-na-na,
pum, pum, pum-na-na."
They sit in their muddy pools
thinking
that candleflies
are shooting stars.

CHICKICHONG

My cheeky chickichong
giddying-up with tipsy butterflies
zigzagging over zinnias.

In the shut-in gallery
I am as free as my brown paper kite
playing with the wind,
tail a crazy thing
without zwill,
without sting,
zingaytaying
in a whistled
breeze.

MAMMIE'S COO-COO AND CALLALOO

Every Sunday
Mammie cook coo-coo and callaloo.

Sometimes, there's
peas and rice and salt-beef stew;

I don't know what I would do
without Mammie's coo-coo and callaloo.

Sometimes there's
chicken with pumkin and dasheen too;

I don't know what I would do
without Mammie's coo-coo and callaloo.

Sometimes there's
pelau, and on the side spicy manicou;

I don't know what I would do
without Mammie's coo-coo and callaloo.

Sometimes there's
poun plantain with curried cascadoo;

I don't know what I would do
without Mammie's coo-coo and callaloo.

Mmmmm, mmmmm I would like some now.
Would you like some too
of Mammie's coo-coo and callaloo?

Yeeeeeeesssssss!!!

I don't know what I would do
without Mammie's coo-coo and callaloo.

MY PRAYING MANTIS

I once had a mantis as a pet.
A praying mantis; you must not forget,

is the tiger of the insect world,
hungry, fierce and extremely bold;

and if you are an insect, keep away
should a mantis be lurking where you play.

Anyway, my mantis was my very best friend.
He sat on my shoulder, and I did defend

his insect's right to stay with me,
protect him from people's curiosity;

for they thought it very strange
the way his body was arranged:

For a start, his neck was very long,
and his heart-shaped head did not belong

to that thin neck and bulbous abdomen
or toothed arms as strong as ten,

wings which gave him speed in flight
when he attacked and with delight

grabbed a cockroach for his supper,
tore and ate it with his choppers.

However, one day, Phoebe, the neighbour's cat,
gobbled up my mantis and that was that.

Phoebe licked her lips, seemed satisfied
with a chewed-up mantis in her inside.

I suppose, for a mantis, the moral to this story
is, look out for cats or you'll be sorry.

Nearly every day was a sunny day in the rural Jamaican village where I grew up. I spent most of my time outdoors. I had my own banana tree, my own pig, my own goat and a hen. When bananas from my tree were sold – or chicks from my hen or kids from my goat – the money was mine. From the age of about six I had jobs before and after school. Up early I would feed the chickens, get water at the standing pipe on the village road, collect firewood or run errands. I'd help to milk the goats or the cow. I'd fetch the horse, the donkey or the mule from some grassy patch where they'd been feeding all night. My village was near the sea and had a running stream. With my four brothers I went fishing from a cliff overhanging the sea and also went

James Berry

to catch shrimps in the stream. We swam in the sea. We picked young coconuts, chopped them open, drank the cooling water and scooped out the young, white and soft jelly coconut and ate it. We played cricket on the beach. We made all the things we played with: the bats, balls, kites, tops, wheels and so on. The first stories that really grabbed me were our Caribbean fun and horror folk tales, Anancy stories, which we told each other at home. As for reading, I had only my school texts, no other story-books or poems. When I came to England, at twenty-three, I was able to feast myself on a world of written poems and stories. My first poem was published when I was thirty-five and I have since written many books of stories and poems.

LETTER FROM YOUR SPECIAL-BIG-PUPPY-DOG

from Scribbled Notes Picked up by Owners and Rewritten because of bad grammar, bad spelling, bad writing

You know I'm so big
I'll soon become a person.
You know I want to know more
of all that you know. Yet
you leave the house, so, so often.
And not one quarrel between us.
Why don't you come home ten times
a day? Come, tell me the way
your boss is bad? See me sit,
listening, sad? And you know,

and I know, it's best
when you first come in.
You call my name. And O
I go starry-eyed on you,
can't stop wagging, jumping,
holding, licking your face,
saying, "D'you know – d'you know –
you're quite, quite a dish!"
Come home – come call my name –
every time thirty minutes pass.

LETTER FROM YOUR KITTEN-CAT-ALMOST-BIG-CAT

You tell me to clear up
the strings of wool off
the floor, just to see how
I slink out the door. But O
you're my mum. Fifty times
big to climb on. You stroke
my back from head to tail.
You tickle my furry throat,
letting my claws needle your side,
and my teeth nibble your hand
till I go quiet. I purr.
I purr like a poor boy
snoring, after gift of a dinner.

I leap into your lap only
to start everything over.

You see, I sign a letter myself PiG.
But O most of all
I want you to see
I want us to dig together,
wallow together and share
one bath. I want us to walk
together, all muddy and smart.
I want you to have
my work and my fun.

Isn't My Name Magical?

Nobody can see my name on me.
My name is inside
and all over me, unseen
like other people also keep it.
Isn't my name magical?

My name is mine only.
It tells I am individual,
the one special person it shakes
when I'm wanted.

Even if someone else answers
for me, my message hangs in air
haunting others, till it stops
with me, the right name.
Isn't your name and my name magic?

If I'm with hundreds of people
and my name gets called,
my sound switches me on to answer
like it was my human electricity.

My name echoes across playground,
it comes, it demands my attention.
I have to find out who calls,
who wants me for what.
My name gets blurted out in class,
it is terror, at a bad time,
because somebody is cross.

My name gets called in a whisper
I am happy, because
my name may have touched me
with a loving voice.
Isn't your name and my name magic?

82

BYE NOW

Walk good
Walk good
Noh mek macca go juk yu
Or cow go buk yu.
Noh mek dog bite yu
Or hungry go ketch yu, yah!

Noh mek sunhot turn yu dry.
Noh mek rain soak yu.
Noh mek tief tief yu.
Or stone go buck yu foot, yah!
Walk good
Walk good

GOODBYE NOW

Walk well
Walk well
Don't let thorns run in you
Or let a cow butt you.
Don't let a dog bite you
Or hunger catch you, hear!

Don't let sun's heat turn you dry.
Don't let rain soak you.
Don't let a thief rob you
Or a stone bump your foot, hear!
Walk well
Walk well

Frank Collymore

 Frank Collymore,
affectionately known as "Colly", died in 1980. But he lives on
in the memory of the Caribbean people for his unique
contribution to West Indian art and literature. A teacher by
profession he was also a painter, actor, writer, poet
and broadcaster, committed to freedom of expression and to
art in all its forms. From the early 1940s, right up until
1975 when he was eighty-two, he edited the literary magazine BIM.
There were times when the future of the magazine was uncertain,
but Colly kept it alive, almost single-handedly. Through his
teaching and letter-writing he was a friend and inspiration to
generations of Caribbean writers, giving them support and advice.
It is said that no letter to Colly ever went unanswered.
Collymore's poetry is light, humorous and full of the simple joys of life.
Above all it encapsulates the warmth and humanity that
he showed to others during his lifetime.

THE ZOBO BIRD

Do you think we skip,
Do you think we hop,
Do you think we flip,
Do you think we flop,
Do you think we trip
This fearful measure
And hop and hip
For personal pleasure?

O no, O no,
We are full of woe
From top to toe:
It's the dread Zobo,
    The Zobo bird.

He brings us bane,
He brings us blight,
He brings us pain
By day and night:
And so we must
Though it take all day
Dance or bust
Till he flies away.

Away, away!
O don't delay.
  Go, Zobo, go,
      O Zobo bird!

PHINNIPHIN

The tide is in,
   The tide is in,
      The Phinniphin
         Are out.

They love the sea,
   The salty sea,
      Of this there is
         No doubt.

O watch them flop
   And slip and slop
      With clumsy hop
         Right past

The sandy beach
   Until they reach
      The friendly sea
         At last.

But when the tide,
   The shifty tide
      Stays right outside
         The bar,

They can't go in
   The Phinniphin;
      The Phinniphin
         Cannot go in:
            They'd have to hop
            Too far.

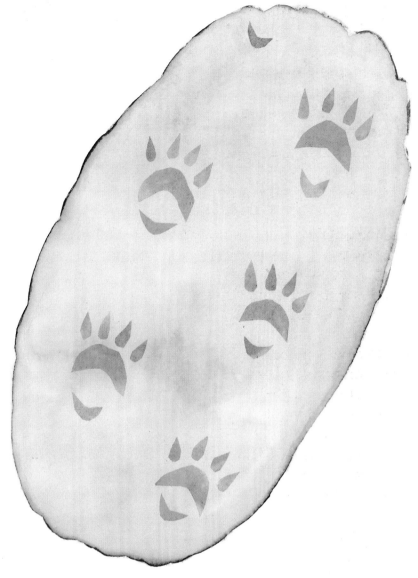

THE SPIDER

I'm told that the spider
Has coiled up inside her
Enough silky material
To spin an aerial
One-way track
to the moon and back;
Whilst I
Cannot even catch a fly

Bibliographies

Opal Palmer Adisa,
Jamaican-born writer, has lived in California since 1979. Her published works are *Travelling Women*, a poetry collection with Devorah Major (Jukebox Press, Oakland, 1986); *Bake-Face and Other Guava Stories* (Kelsey Street Press, Berkeley, 1986) and *Pina, the Many-Eyed Fruit* (Julian Richardson Associate, San Francisco, 1985). Her poetry has appeared in many anthologies including *Caribbean Poetry Now* edited by Steward Brown (Hodder & Stoughton). Opal Palmer Adisa has written plays which have been produced in the Bay Area, and has taught at San Francisco State University. She is also a storyteller of Caribbean and African tales.

John Agard
was born in Guyana but has lived in Britain since 1977. He was attached to the Commonwealth Institute as a touring speaker for eight years during which time he visited some two thousand schools all across the UK talking about his Caribbean experience. His adult collection *Man to Pan* won the 1982 Casa de Las Americas Cuban Poetry Award. His other adult collections include *Mangoes and Bullets* and a book of love poems, *Lovelines for a Goat-born Lady*, published by Serpent's Tail. Among his many children's books are *I Din Do Nuttin*, *Laughter Is an Egg* and *The Emperor's Dan-Dan*, a picture book calypso retelling of *The Emperor's New Clothes*. He has also written plays for children.

James Berry
was born in a Jamaican coastal village and was among the early Caribbean settlers to Britain. He became involved with black people's cultural life from early on in the UK while steadily developing his writing, both for children and adults. He reads internationally, has broadcast on radio and television and conducted writers' workshops in schools over the years. Among his awards, his children's book *A Thief in the Village* won him the Smarties Prize for Children's Books and *When I Dance* the Signal Poetry Award. *Fractured Circles* and *Chain of Days* are among his adult poetry collections and he has also written a collection of stories for children, *Anancy Spiderman*. James won first prize in the Poetry Society's National Competition of 1981.

Valerie Bloom
was born in Clarendon, Jamaica, where she worked as a librarian before training as a teacher. She completed an Honours degree in English with African and Caribbean studies at the University of Kent, Canterbury, and later worked as Multicultural Arts Officer with North West Arts in Manchester. Her first book of poetry *Touch Mi, Tell Mi* was published in 1983 by Bogle L'Ouverture, and the revised edition in 1990. Her book of children's poems, *Duppy Jamboree*, was published by Cambridge University Press in 1992 and she has had poems published in several anthologies.

Dionne Brand
was born in Trinidad but now lives in Toronto, Canada. She has published six books of poetry – *Fore Day Morning, Earth Magic* (children's poetry), *Winter Epigrams, Primitive Offensive, Chronicles of the Hostile Sun* and *No Language is Neutral*, which was nominated for the 1990 Governor General's Awards. She has also co-authored a work of non-fiction, *Rivers Have Sources Trees Have Roots – Speaking of Racism*, and a book of short stories *Sans Souci and Other Stories*. Her latest book of non-fiction *No Burden to Carry, Narratives of Black Working Women in Ontario 1920s to 1950s* is a collection of oral histories.

David Campbell
is a songwriter, poet and singer. He was born and raised in Guyana, South America, but is now a Canadian citizen living in Vancouver, British Colombia. He has performed in concert and on radio and television in Britain, Europe and North America. David Campbell has written over one thousand songs, many of which have been recorded in albums such as *Through Arawak Eyes, Underneath the Blue Canadian Sky* and *Song*. His poems have appeared in his books of song lyrics. He has worked widely among the indigenous people of the Americas.

Faustin Charles
was born in Trinidad and came to Britain in 1962. He has had three collections of poetry published – *The Expatriate* in 1969, *Crab Track* in 1973 and *Days and Nights in the Magic Forest*. He has also written two novels and a book of West Indian folk-tales as well as books for children. He was a visiting lecturer for the Commonwealth Institute and has edited a collection of folk-tales from around the Caribbean – *Under the Storyteller's Spell*.

Frank Collymore

was born in Barbados in January 1893. He was a teacher and editor of the literary magazine BIM, to which he contributed numerous poems, short stories, plays, literary reviews and articles. He published several collections of poetry, including *Thirty Poems* (1944), *Beneath the Casuarinas* (1945), *Flotsam* (1948), *Collected Poems* (1959) and *Selected Poems* (1971). Frank Collymore died in July 1980. He is remembered by Barbadians as one of the island's greatest ever champions of literature and the arts.

John Lyons

is a Trinidadian-born painter and poet who has exhibited extensively, both nationally and internationally. He emigrated to England in 1959 and studied painting at Goldsmiths College, London and at the University of Newcastle-upon-Tyne. He won the Peterloo Afro-Caribbean/Asian poetry prize on two occasions and was commended in the Poetry Society's National Poetry Competition. His first collection of poems, *Lure of the Cascadura*, was published by Bogle L'Ouverture in 1989. He is also one of four poets in a collection called *The Sun Rises in the North* (Smith/Doorstop Books, 1991).

Marc Matthews

is a Guyanese storyteller-poet-dramatist. His first collection published by Karnak House, *Guyana My Altar*, won the Guyana First Publication award in 1987. His most recent collection, published by People Tree Press, is titled *A Season of Sometimes*. He was an original member of the All-Ah-We team who, between 1973 and 1978, toured eleven Caribbean countries and made 160 performances. He has appeared in plays and feature films. He is now living in Guyana again after a number of years in the UK.

Pamela Mordecai

was born in Jamaica. Two of her children's books have been published: *Storypoems – a First Collection* (Ginn, 1987) and *Don't Ever Wake a Snake* (Sandberry Press, 1992). *Journey Poem*, a collection for adults, appeared in 1988. A Language Arts teacher, she has written or co-written some fifteen books for the Caribbean. In 1980 she was awarded the Institute of Jamaica's Tercentenary Medal for her writing. In 1993 her collection, *Ezra's Goldfish and Other Story-poems* won Jamaica's first Vic Reid Award for Children's Literature. She lives in Kingston where she and her husband, Martin, run Sandberry Press. They have three children.

Grace Nichols

was born in Guyana but has lived in Britain since 1977. Her publications for children include two collections of short stories: *Trust You Wriggly* and *Leslyn in London*, and a popular collection of poems, *Come On Into My Tropical Garden* (A&C Black). *I Is A Long Memoried Woman*, her first adult book of poems, won the 1983 Commonwealth Poetry Prize. Her other collections, *The Fat Black Woman's Poems* and *Lazy Thoughts of a Lazy Woman*, are both published by Virago along with her first novel, *Whole of a Morning Sky*. She has performed her poetry widely throughout Britain and abroad and has worked with both radio and television.

Telcine Turner

was born on New Providence Island, in the Bahamas. Her publications include a collection of poems for children, *Song of the Surreys* (Macmillan Caribbean, 1977); a full-length play, *Woman Take Two* (Vantage Press, New York, 1987); edited stories for children, *Once Below A Time* (Macmillan Caribbean, 1988), and edited stories and poems for schools, *Climbing Clouds* (Macmillan Caribbean 1988). She is married to the Bahamian artist, James O Rolle, and currently teaches at the College of the Bahamas.

Index of First Lines

MORE WALKER PAPERBACKS
For You to Enjoy

SOUTH AND NORTH, EAST AND WEST
The Oxfam Book of Children's Stories edited by Michael Rosen

Animal stories from Botswana and Indonesia, ghost stories from Jamaica and Vietnam, family stories from India and South Africa, a creation myth from Brazil... Each of these twenty-five tales is illustrated by an internationally acclaimed artist. All royalties benefit the work of Oxfam.

"A kaleidoscopic collection of stories from all round the world... A great book for reading aloud, or alone." *The Guardian*

0-7445-4366-5   £7.99

OUT AND ABOUT
by Shirley Hughes

Eighteen richly illustrated poems portray the weather and activities associated with the various seasons.

"Hughes at her best. Simple, evocative rhymes conjure up images that then explode in the magnificent richness of her paintings." *The Guardian*

0-7445-1422-3   £4.99

A CUP OF STARSHINE
compiled by Jill Bennett, illustrated by Graham Percy

In this lively anthology for young children you'll find poems about subjects as diverse as washing and springtime, playing and the moon...

"A beautifully produced and illustrated anthology." *Independent on Sunday*

0-7445-3040-7   £5.99

BIRDS, BEASTS AND FISHES
compiled by Anne Carter, illustrated by Reg Cartwright

Over fifty poems on creatures of all shapes and sizes, colours and character by some of the finest poets from across the ages – from Aesop to Blake, Edward Lear to Ted Hughes.

"Wonderfully bold, colourful, naive and witty pictures... A lovely book." *The School Librarian*

0-7445-3056-3   £6.99